An Aboriginal Family

LIBRARY OF CONGRESS CATALOGING IN PUBLICATION DATA

Browne, Rollo.
  An aboriginal family.

  Summary: An eleven-year-old Aboriginal girl describes
her life with her family on a former cattle station in
the Northern Territory of Australia.
    1. Australian aborigines—Australia—Northern Territory
—Social life and customs—Juvenile literature.
    [1. Australian aborigines—Australia—Northern Territory—
Social life and customs] I. Fairclough, Chris, ill.
II. Title.
GN667.N6B76   1985   994.29'0049915   84-19447
ISBN 0-8225-1655-1 (lib. bdg.)

Manufactured in the United States of America

    3   4   5   6   7   8   9   10   94   93   92   91

An Aboriginal Family

Rollo Browne
Photographs by Chris Fairclough

⌊ Lerner Publications Company · Minneapolis

Lynette Joshua, 11, lives in the Northern Territory of Australia. Australia is divided into six states and two territories. The other territory is Canberra, which is the country's capital. In some ways, Canberra is like Washington, D.C.

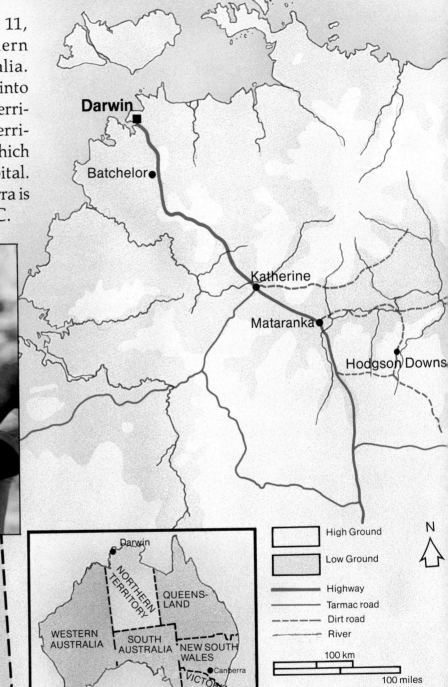

Darwin

Batchelor

Katherine

Mataranka

Hodgson Downs

Darwin

NORTHERN TERRITORY

QUEENS-LAND

WESTERN AUSTRALIA

SOUTH AUSTRALIA

NEW SOUTH WALES

VICTORIA

Canberra

TASMANIA

N

| High Ground |
| Low Ground |
| Highway |
| Tarmac road |
| Dirt road |
| River |

100 km

100 miles

Lynette has two older sisters, Mildred and Lillian, and two younger sisters, Sandra and Rosemary. She also has a brother, Lancen. They all live with their parents at the camp on Hodgson Downs Cattle Station. Before it was closed down, the station was a big cattle farm.

The camp is called Minyerri and was named after the big billabong, or waterhole, near the camp. They call it "the camp" because Aboriginal people camped there when the cattle station was first started in 1885.

Hodgson Downs is about 372 miles (600 kilometers) from Darwin, the capital of the Northern Territory. Mataranka is the town nearest the camp. It's about 100 miles (160 kilometers) away. You can take a bus from Darwin to Mataranka, but no buses run out to Hodgson Downs. To get there, you have to find a ride.

There are no telephones in the camp, but there is a two-way radio. Every morning at 7:30 A.M., Lynette's father turns on the radio. Then the whole camp listens for their call. "Victor Mike eight Lima Lima, Minyerri Community come in please." That's the way Outpost Radio in Darwin calls the camp.

During the wet season, it rains a lot and the roads are often flooded. Then the radio is the only way the camp can get help or send messages. The wet season begins in late December and lasts for about four months. Then it stops raining and the dry season begins. The rivers stop running and dry up into billabongs.

About 80 people live in the camp. The camp has 15 houses, a big store shed, a meeting shed, a clinic, and a shower block.

Lynette's family lives in a house built from timber, corrugated iron, and concrete. All the houses in the camp are like that. Most of the houses have one room with a veranda at the front. Families spend most of their time outside on the shady veranda or down by the billabong.

Lynette's mother does all the cooking outside. The family gets up early every morning and her mother makes tea and damper for breakfast.

To make damper, she mixes flour, baking powder, salt, and water into a smooth dough. Then she pats the dough into little round flat cakes. The dampers are put into the fire and covered with hot ashes. Soon they are cooked.

Sometimes Lynette's mother makes bread in a camp oven. This is a big iron pot that sits in the fire. It has a special lid she covers with hot coals. The bread tastes good but it takes a long time to make.

After breakfast, the older children go to school. Then Lynette's mother collects firewood and does other chores. Sometimes she goes down to the billabong to look for wild foods. When she's not busy, she likes to play cards or talk to friends or relatives.

All the water used by the family for washing and drinking is pumped from the billabong. The clothes are washed at the faucet outside the house or down at the billabong.

When she is not at school, Lynette often helps her mother with the cleaning. She also helps take care of her little sister.

All the children in the camp go to Minyerri School. The school is held in two trailers near the camp and has only two classes. Lynette and the older children are in the primary class, and Sandra is in the infants class.

The school's two teachers live in a trailer near the school. There is also an Aboriginal assistant teacher who lives in the camp. She usually teaches the very youngest children who don't speak much English.

Most of the people in the camp belong to the Alawa tribe. The old people still speak the Alawa language. Not many children speak Alawa, but most are able to understand it. Families usually speak *Kriol*, or Aboriginal English, to each other.

At school Lynette and her friends study English, math, science, and other subjects. They also get to play on the school trampoline. Sometimes one of the older people in the camp comes to the school to give Alawa lessons. Usually, though, children learn Alawa from their relatives.

Although the camp has no electricity, there is an electricity generator at the school. Everyone goes there to watch films, which are shown against the trailer wall.

The men from Minyerri camp used to work for Hodgson Downs Cattle Station. Now that the station has closed down, there is no work for any of these men. They must try to make money in other ways.

Some of the men make and sell boomerangs. Lynette's uncle makes didgeridoos and sells them to shops in the towns. A didgeridoo is a long, hollowed-out tree branch. When blown like a horn, it makes a low droning sound.

The men play didgeridoos and clap sticks together to make *corrobore* music. *Corrobore* is the word Aborigines use to describe their dancing and singing. The men and women always dance separately, and sometimes the dancers paint themselves with white clay.

Before the *mununga*, or white people, came to the area, the land belonged to the Alawa. Lynette's grandmother has told her stories about the land. She says that the country was made during the Dreamtime by spirits who traveled across the land.

12

The Alawa believe that the Minyerri billabong was made by Wadjurndu, the Goanna Spirit. They say that the billabong is part of the Goanna Dreaming. No one is allowed to fire a rifle into the water. As long as anyone can remember, the billabong has never dried up. People at the camp stay there so they can be close to their country and look after dreaming places like the billabong. 13

At the end of the dry season, the Alawas have "ceremony time." Aborigines have ceremonies to renew their links with the Dreamtime spirits who made the land. They call this their dreaming.

Some ceremonies are secret and religious. They are often only for men or for women. At other times, anyone can join in.

People are linked to their land through dreaming and they are linked to each other through "skin groups." Every Alawa person belongs to a skin group.

The Alawa tribe has eight different skin groups. Each skin group has one name for women and another for men.

Someone's skin name depends on his or her mother's skin name. Lynette's mother's skin name is Nangari, so she and her sisters are Nangala skin and her brother is Jangala skin. Even little children know their skin names.

Everyone in a skin group is part of the same family, whether or not they are related. Lynette calls all the women in her mother's skin group "mother" and all the men in her father's skin group "father."

Two years ago, Lynette's father took a job as assistant teacher at the Minyerri School. To train for the job, he went to the Aboriginal Teacher Education College in Batchelor. Batchelor is between Hodgson Downs and Darwin. Because it is so far from the camp, the whole family went with him.

There they lived in a house near the college. Everyone in the family enjoyed this new experience. The house had a modern kitchen with an electric stove and a refrigerator, an inside toilet, and beds for each person.

16

While their father was at college, the children went to Batchelor School. It was much bigger than Minyerri School and had a playground with two trampolines.

There were other Aboriginal children at the school, too. Their parents were also attending the college.

On weekends, the Joshuas sometimes went shopping in Darwin. They liked to look at the clothes and always found something to buy. Lynette also enjoyed watching all the different cars.

In the middle of the dry season, Lynette's father finished his training. The family went home to Hodgson Downs and her father was chosen to be president of Minyerri.

Now that Lynette's father is president of the camp, it's his job to order food. The food is sent from Katherine, a town about 160 miles (260 kilometers) away. He orders all the food by radio.

Before the camp had a radio, it sometimes ran out of food. Then the people in the camp would go hungry until a message could reach Katherine. That doesn't happen anymore.

In the dry season, a truck brings supplies from Katherine every two weeks. When the truck arrives, Lynette's father divides the food. Most people in the camp help pay for the supplies. They order flour, sugar, tea, salt, baking powder, milk powder, and cans of fruit and meat. The truck also brings matches, tobacco, bullets, and other items.

In the wet season when the roads are blocked, the camp orders enough food to last for four months. One year the truck couldn't cross one of the streams. The driver had to turn back and leave everything in Roper Valley, almost 30 miles (45 kilometers) from Minyerri. Some of the men took the new camp tractor to get the supplies. They brought everything back on the trailer and stacked it in the store shed.

The camp doesn't need to order all its food from Katherine. People collect a lot of food from the bush, or countryside, around the camp. This food is called bush-tucker.

The men often go out hunting for kangaroo, turkey, or goanna, which are big lizards. They use rifles or shotguns if they have them. Otherwise they use spears.

Cattle still live on the land around the station. Some of them, called "cleanskins," are wild and have never been branded. Every two weeks a steer is killed and the meat is shared by everyone in the camp. They call this "the killer."

On the day of the killer, the men go out early in the morning. They ride on the back of a truck and take a rifle, butcher's knives, and an ax. They bring all the meat back to the camp. None of the meat from the killer is wasted.

If there is meat left over, the people rub coarse salt into it and hang it up to dry. Then it is stored to be eaten later.

In the dry season, there are fish in the streams and waterholes. Two kinds of fish, bream and catfish, are small. Another kind, barrimundi, is so big that one makes a meal for a whole family. There are also turtles and small freshwater crocodiles, which are caught with fishing hooks and bait. Turtle meat is very sweet.

Lynette goes out hunting for goanna with her mother and the other women. They chase the water goannas right under the water or dig the sand goannas out of their holes. Once they found a big goanna by the road on the way to the fishing hole. Lynette's Aunt Cleo saw it first and so it belonged to her, even though someone else killed it.

The women get a lot of bush-tucker from the billa-bongs. They gather the stems and seed pods from water-lily plants and collect freshwater mussels and crayfish. All of the children learn how to find things to eat by going out into the bush with their families. At the end of the wet season they can find many kinds of fruit, including white currants and black plums. They pick up the ripe plums from around the trees and then throw sticks to knock more plums off the branches.

Wild honey is one of the best kinds of bush-tucker. The Aborigines call it "sugerbag." To find the honey, Lynette and her friends follow little black bees back to their tree. Then they cut into the tree to open up the hive. The bees don't even sting them.

Many useful things besides food are found in the bush. Soap berries are used for washing hands, and bushes are used for making brooms. Paints are made from different clays and rocks. Some of the old people make medicines from plants. These medicines can cure headaches, colds, cuts, and sores.

One of the houses at the camp is used as a government clinic. Mary, the health worker, keeps medicine there. Anyone can come in to see her at any time.

Every six weeks, a doctor flies out to Hodgson Downs. The airstrip is about 4 miles (6 kilometers) from the camp and someone must drive out to meet the doctor. If a person is very sick, the "flying doctor" is called by radio and makes a special trip.

Lynette's Aunt Rosie was very sick during the wet season one year. The roads were flooded and no one could get to the airstrip to pick up the doctor. Her aunt had to swim two streams and walk a long way through the mud to meet the plane. The doctor took her to the hospital in Katherine. When she was better, Rosie came back to Minyerri.

There are many children at the camp, and Lynette and her sisters and brother have a lot of friends. Lynette likes to play marbles, softball, and basketball. She also enjoys a game called three-can. To play three-can, one person knocks over a pile of cans with a ball. That person must then stand all three cans back on top of each other before anyone else hits him or her with the ball.

After school, Lynette and her friends often go swimming in the billabong. Sometimes they go instead to the waterhole at Bella Glen, a little under 10 miles (15 kilometers) away.

At the beginning of the wet season, the weather is very hot. After the first rains, the rivers and streams fill with water. Then Lynette and her friends can cool off in the nearby waterfalls or slide down the rocks. Sometimes they paint themselves with the clay on the riverbanks or use it to make models.

Some people in the camp enjoy traveling around to work or to visit relatives. Lynette liked seeing Darwin and Batchelor, but she was glad to come home. As she says, "It's always good to be back in your own country."

Dreaming:
The Aborigine's Religion

Dreaming is an English word used to describe the Aborigines' beliefs about their country and how it was created.

Aborigines believe that the world was created during the **Dreamtime**, when **Dreamtime spirits** walked over the land and made the countryside, plants, animals, and people. These spirits took various shapes, including those of people and animals. After the Dreamtime, the spirits sank back into the earth.

The special places where events happened during the Dreamtime and where the Dreamtime spirits returned into the earth are called **Dreaming places**. The Aborigines believe that the Dreamtime spirits still remain at the Dreaming places.

As part of their religion, Aborigines have **ceremonies** in which they often sing and dance. They usually hold the ceremonies at special Dreaming places. Aboriginal people believe that during ceremonies they can get in touch with the Dreamtime spirits.

Facts about Aborigines

Aborigines were the first people to live in Australia and have been there for at least 40,000 years. When European settlers came to Australia about two hundred years ago, there were about 500 different tribes like the Alawas. Each tribe had its own language.

There are about 206,000 Aborigines living in Australia. Only about one-third of these people are full-blooded Aborigines like the Joshuas. Some Aborigines, like Lynette and her family, still live in the same area that their ancestors have always lived in. They have not married outside their tribe or mixed with the other Australians.

Yet most Aborigines are of mixed ancestry—part Aboriginal and part European. Many of these people now live in the cities of Australia.

NORTH
AMERICA

SOUTH
AMERICA

EUROPE

A S I A

AFRICA

AUSTRALIA

Aboriginal lands

Families the World Over

Some children in foreign countries live like you do. Others live very differently. In these books, you can meet children from all over the world. You'll learn about their games and schools, their families and friends, and what it's like to grow up in a faraway land.

Lerner Publications Company, 241 First Avenue North, Minneapolis, Minnesota 55401